ANGELS

The Beauty of Silent Messengers

This edition first published in 2005 by
New Holland Publishers (UK) Ltd
London • Cape Town • Sydney • Auckland

10 9 8 7 6 5 4 3 2 1

www.newhollandpublishers.com

Garfield House
86–88 Edgware Road
London W2 2EA
United Kingdom

ISBN 1 84537 290 5

Publishing Manager	Jo Hemmings
Senior Editor	Kate Michell
Assistant Editor	Kate Parker
Translator	Christine Shuttleworth

	©	Elisabeth Sandmann Verlag GmbH, München
		2. edition 2005
		Alle Rechte vorbehalten
Photographs		Clemens Zahn
Essay		Cees Nooteboom
Afterword		Claudia Lanfranconi
Editorial		Eva Römer
Design		Georg Feigl
Production		Karin Mayer, Peter Karg-Cordes
Lithography		inteca Media Service GmbH, Rosenheim
Printing and Binding		L.E.G.O., Vicenza

ANGELS

The Beauty of Silent Messengers

NEW
HOLLAND

Cees Nooteboom

The Angels Return

Suddenly, they are here again: the angels. They have returned, even if we hadn't noticed them disappear. The whole time they had been near to us, in cemeteries, on the capitals of Romanesque churches, in Filippo Lippi's paintings, as sculptures by Bernini, in the words of Rilke, Shakespeare and Dante. Nothing had really happened to the angels; they had waited calmly for centuries, in Chartres Cathedral, in Rembrandt's prints and in Milton's *Paradise Lost*. They were waiting for us to see them again, to think about them again. They had the time that we were about to lose.

When did I last think about angels? Or did I never really think about them, because I had them around me from my earliest childhood days? They were everywhere, in prayer books, devotional pictures, paintings, stained-glass windows. If you were brought up as a Catholic you could hardly escape them. An angel announced to Mary that she was to be the Mother of God, an angel with a flaming sword drove Adam and Eve out of paradise, Jacob fought with an angel, Lucifer was a fallen angel, and, if things were as they should be, we each had a guardian angel who was supposed to protect us from all possible disaster.

Angels, we also learned, were of different kinds, seraphim and cherubim, thrones and powers, ordinary angels and archangels. The suggestion was that they were men, admittedly men in almost feminine attire, and in a mysterious way they were never old – a 50-year-old angel was unthinkable. They had locks rather than hair, no shoes, and certainly not spectacles. They also had this peculiar anatomical addition, wings, which should really have put them in the ornithological category. Yet, despite all their feathers, they did seem to belong to the human race and thus to the mammals; an almost blasphemous thought, because they were too holy, too different and too timeless. But were they really men or not?

Not, according to the second Council of Nicaea in 787, simply because they have no bodies. And the Koran is quite sure about this too. They have not a single attribute of the male or female sex, which strictly speaking need not mean that they have no bodies, but does rather increase the problem. There is always a moment when something quite everyday suddenly becomes a puzzle, an enigma that can only be overcome by means of silly questions. Has anyone ever

seen the skeleton of an angel? Has anyone ever tried to draw an angel's skeleton? I can imagine that Leonardo da Vinci, who was so interested in the science of flying, must have tried it, if only to find out how those wings are actually anatomically fixed to the body.

Angels are imaginary beings, but although, according to the Council of Nicaea, they have no bodies, this circumstance has clearly not prevented anyone from portraying them with bodies – a shadow might be cast across the airspace by all the winged messengers of Raphael, Giotto, Fra Angelico, Rubens and Zurbarán, and whole squadrons could be recruited from all the angels who guard the dead until the Day of Judgement in Spanish and Italian cemeteries.

I particularly remember the burial of St Catherine by Zurbarán, in which three gigantic, very masculine angels manoeuvre the body of the saint, wrapped in a silken shroud, past the horrifying instrument of martyrdom, bristling with knives, on which she met her death. This image conveys an impression of silence, but of course that is not possible. There must have been a mighty flapping and rustling of wings to be heard, as the

angels tried not to get in each other's way and at the same time made sure they did not lose their balance.

One wonders what sort of feathers these actually are, how much air is displaced by the angels with their full-sized wings, how fast they fly, how they land, whether they have problems with storms, air currents and other weather; in short, puzzles that have something to do with aerodynamics as well as holiness.

Why are we so fascinated by these holy dream-figures? Precisely because they are dream-figures, who can do something we would love to do ourselves – fly. They do not need to worry about the laws of gravity to which we are subject; they fly unburdened between our earthly transience and the eternity that is their habitat. Despite their weightlessness, they do not need to wear the clothing, unworthy of man, that our mortal astronauts have to don to be able to travel only a very little distance away from the Earth that continually calls us and them to return. Anyone who has ever flown in a dream knows what I mean. It is not the same as in a ski-lift, a helicopter or an aircraft, it is a question of independent flight, of a slow beating of wings, the

strange swaying, floating and blissfully gliding along on a current of air that we have copied from the seagulls, buzzards and storks. It is a sensual feeling of power, the view from high above our world, where we can catch sight of everything, even what is most hidden.

I have tried to imagine what it would be like to meet an angel. One must stand in front of one of those marble angels in the cemetery of Genoa or of San Michele in Venice and imagine that he (for of course angels are male – after all, they have names like Gabriel and Michael) is smoothing out his marble wings and spreading them out. Then, when he lifts them, ready to fly away, you suddenly find yourself standing in the shadow of a solar eclipse. You have been put in your place, the place where you belong if you cannot fly and do not live in heaven.

Now imagine for a moment that you are the Virgin Mary. You are sitting quietly in your room, suspecting nothing, the Magnificat has not yet begun and nobody has told you anything. Then an angel arrives, a heavenly messenger, for whom the stratosphere is no more than a threshold. Suddenly you hear the rustle of those

wings, as though a prehistoric bird were about to land. Have you ever thought about what that must sound like? Think about when a pigeon flies past, and imagine how it must be when the wings are a hundred times as large as a pigeon's.

The painter Sandro Botticelli has seen this moment of meeting with the power of his imagination. A red floor with square stone slabs, a severe pattern, geometric lines as a contrast to all the swirling textiles, the folds and breaks in the garments (angels are rarely naked) of the woman and her winged visitor. At this moment, for both of them, the world no longer exists. Eternity is at work here.

It is deathly quiet. The messenger has just arrived, he has knelt down and stretched out his right hand to the woman, who stands bending slightly over him. Their hands are almost touching; the image is one of stunning intimacy – angels and humans never normally come so close to each other. Both have all their fingers spread out, as though that is the language in which they want to express themselves, for no words have yet been uttered. Do angels speak all languages? And what do

they actually think of us? Are we failures who cannot fly, who do not know how to live for ever, who have never seen God? Perhaps they even pity us, and why not? But this angel does not need to pity Mary.

She does not look at him; if she did, she would see the fear that lives within his reverence for her. I think that most people who gaze at a picture such as this do not give serious thought to the lunacy of this message. A man with wings has just flown, like a human aircraft, into a small Renaissance chamber. His wings are still gently raised, the landscape outside with its one sparse, tall tree lies there indifferently in the Mediterranean light. The angel is about to convey a message from a world millions of miles away, yet for him bafflingly close, an unattainable realm in which time and distance do not exist.

Messengers, couriers, envoys, representatives of a dream world: because we wanted them to exist, we created angels. Out of words, ink, silver and gold, ivory and wood, marble and porcelain, we created them, so as to be able to believe for a moment that it was possible, with a few beats of our wings, to rise above life

on earth and fly without time in the realm of time. But no, says the poet Czeslaw Milosz, that cannot be so. He has heard a voice that proclaims the opposite, that it was not us who created angels, and perhaps a time has come when we would rather believe him to be right. The darkness that has once again fallen over the world reminds us of earlier times, when peace and survival were as little to be taken for granted as they are today, and humankind, like the old poets, wanted to believe in angels, so as not to be alone on the earth.

Missen, April 2004

At night, methought, in dream
A shape of speechless beauty did appear;
It stood like light on a careering stream
Of golden clouds which shook the atmosphere;
A wingèd youth, his radiant brow did wear
The Morning Star; a wild dissolving bliss
Over my frame he breathed, approaching near,
And bent his eyes of kindling tenderness
Near mine, and on my lips impressed a lingering kiss

From The Revolt of Islam: A Poem in Twelve Cantos. First Canto.
Percy Bysshe Shelley, 1792–1822

When I consider every thing that grows
Holds in perfection but a little moment.
That this huge stage presenteth nought but shows
Whereon the stars in secret influence comment.
When I perceive that men as plants increase,
Cheerèd and checked even by the self-same sky,
Vaunt in their youthful sap, at height decrease,
And wear their brave state out of memory;
Then the conceit of this inconstant stay,
Sets you most rich in youth before my sight,
Where wasteful Time debateth with decay
To change your day of youth to sullied night;
And all in war with Time for love of you,
As he takes from you, I engraft you new.

Sonnet 15: When I consider every thing that grows
William Shakespeare, 1564–1616

Under the eye of my beloved Spirit I glide:

O joy! for ever, ever, joy!

I am not hurried – the whole of eternity is mine

From By The Shore
Edward Carpenter, 1844–1929

We see them not – we cannot hear
   The music of their wing –
Yet know we that they sojourn near,
   The Angels of the spring!

They glide along this lovely ground
   When the first violet grows;
Their graceful hands have just unbound
   The zone of yonder rose.

I gather it for thy dear breast,
   From stain and shadow free:
That which an Angel's touch hath blest
   Is meet, my love, for thee!

Are they not all Ministering Spirits?
Robert Stephen Hawker, 1804–75

When Contemplation, like the night-calm felt
Through earth and sky, spreads widely, and sends deep
Into the soul its tranquillising power,
Even then I sometimes grieve for thee, O Man,
Earth's paramount Creature!

From The Prelude, Book Five
William Wordsworth, 1770–1850

Elected Silence, sing to me
And beat upon my whorlèd ear,
Pipe me to pastures still and be
The music that I care to hear.

From The Habit of Perfection
Gerard Manley Hopkins, 1844–89

She walks in beauty like the night
Of cloudless climes and starry skies;
And all that's best of dark and bright
Meets in her aspect and her eyes:
Thus mellow'd to that tender light
Which heaven to gaudy day denies.

One shade the more, one ray the less,
Had half impair'd the nameless grace
Which waves in every raven tress,
Or softly lightens o'er her face –
Where thoughts serenely sweet express
How pure, how dear their dwelling-place.

And on that cheek, and o'er that brow,
So soft, so calm, yet eloquent,
The smiles that win, the tints that glow,
But tells in days of goodness spent,
A mind at peace with all below,
A heart whose love is innocent.

She Walks in Beauty
George Gordon, Lord Byron, 1788–1824

O, let me be alone a while,
No human form is nigh.
And may I sing and muse aloud,
No mortal ear is by.
Away! ye dreams of earthly bliss,
Ye earthly cares begone:
Depart! ye restless wandering thoughts,
And let me be alone!

From Retirement
Anne Brontë, 1820–49

Fair quiet, have I found thee here,
And Innocence thy Sister dear!
Mistaken long, I sought you then
In busie Companies of Men.
Your sacred Plants, if here below,
Only among the Plants will grow.
Society is all but rude,
To this delicious Solitude.

From The Garden
Andrew Marvell, 1621–78

Bright star, would I were stedfast as thou art —
Not in lone splendour hung aloft the night
And watching, with eternal lids apart,
Like nature's patient, sleepless Eremite,
The moving waters at their priestlike task
Of pure ablution round earth's human shores,
Or gazing on the new soft-fallen mask
Of snow upon the mountains and the moors —
No — yet still stedfast, still unchangeable,
Pillow'd upon my fair love's ripening breast,
To feel for ever its soft fall and swell,
Awake for ever in a sweet unrest,
Still, still to hear her tender-taken breath,
And so live ever — or else swoon to death.

Bright Star
John Keats, 1795–1821

Angel, king of streaming morn;
Cherub, call'd by Heav'n to shine;
T' orient tread the waste forlorn;
Guide ætherial, pow'r divine;
    Thou, Lord of all within!

Golden spirit, lamp of day,
Host, that dips in blood the plain,
Bids the crimson'd mead be gay,
Bids the green blood burst the vein;
    Thou, Lord of all within!

Soul, that wraps the globe in light;
Spirit, beckoning to arise;
Drives the frowning brow of night,
Glory bursting o'er the skies;
    Thou, Lord of all within!

Sun
Henry Rowe, 1750–1819

Go, sit upon the lofty hill,
And turn your eyes around,
Where waving woods and waters wild
Do hymn an autumn sound.
The summer sun is faint on them –
The summer flowers depart –
Sit still – as all transform'd to stone,
Except your musing heart.

From The Autumn
Elizabeth Barrett Browning, 1806–61

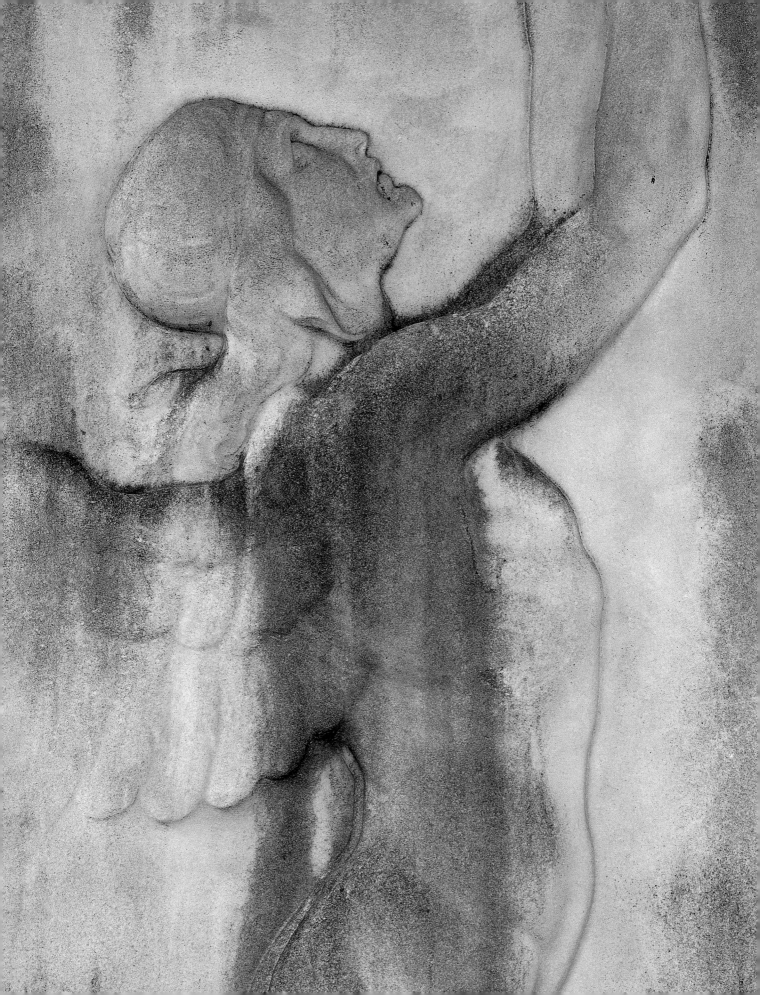

What, O Eternity,
Is Time to thee? –
What to the boundless All
My portion small?

From An Interpreter
John Bannister Tabb, 1845–1909

When to the sessions of sweet silent thought
I summon up remembrance of things past,
I sigh the lack of many a thing I sought,
And with old woes new wail my dear time's waste.
Then can I drown an eye, unused to flow,
For precious friends hid in death's dateless night,
And weep afresh love's long since cancelled woe,
And moan th' expense of many a vanished sight.
Then can I grieve at grievances foregone,
And heavily from woe to woe tell o'er
The sad account of fore-bemoanèd moan,
Which I new pay as if not paid before.
But if the while I think on thee, dear friend,
All losses are restored and sorrows end.

Sonnet 30: When to the sessions of sweet silent thought
William Shakespeare, 1564–1616

Trennung
ist unser Loos
Wiedersehen
unsere
Hoffnung.

A thing of beauty is a joy for ever:
Its loveliness increases; it will never
Pass into nothingness; but still will keep
A bower quiet for us, and a sleep
Full of sweet dreams, and health, and quiet breathing.
Therefore, on every morrow, are we wreathing
A flowery band to bind us to the earth,
Spite of despondence, of the inhuman dearth
Of noble natures, of the gloomy days,
Of all the unhealthy and o'er-darkned ways
Made for our searching: yes, in spite of all,
Some shape of beauty moves away the pall
From our dark spirits. Such the sun, the moon,
Trees old and young, sprouting a shady boon
For simple sheep; and such are daffodils
With the green world they live in; and clear rills
That for themselves a cooling covert make
'Gainst the hot season; the mid-forest brake,
Rich with a sprinkling of fair musk-rose blooms:
And such too is the grandeur of the dooms
We have imagined for the mighty dead;
All lovely tales that we have read or heard:
An endless fountain of immortal drink,
Pouring unto us from the heaven's brink.

From Endymion, Book One
John Keats, 1795–1821

Eve shall kiss night,

And the leaves stir like rain

As the wind stealeth light

O'er the grass of the plain.

Unseen are thine eyes

Mid the dreamy night's sleeping,

And on my mouth there lies

The dear rain of thy weeping.

Hold silence, love, speak not of the sweet day departed,

Cling close to me, love, lest I waken sad-hearted!

O kind day, O dear day, short day, come again!

From Love is Enough: Song VII: Dawn Talks to Day
William Morris, 1834–96

Come then under the trees, where the leaf-cloths
    Curtain us in so dark
That here we're safe from even the ermin-moth's
    Flitting remark.

Here in this swarthy, secret tent,
    Where black boughs flap the ground,
You shall draw the thorn from my discontent,
    Surgeon me sound.

This rare, rich night! For in here
    Under the yew-tree tent
The darkness is loveliest where I could sear
    You like frankincense into scent.

From Liaison
D.H. Lawrence, 1885–1930

And ask ye why these sad tears stream?
Why these wan eyes are dim with weeping?
I had a dream – a lovely dream,
Of her that in the grave is sleeping.

I saw her as 'twas yesterday,
The bloom upon her cheek still glowing;
And round her play'd a golden ray,
And on her brows were gay flowers blowing.

With angel-hand she swept a lyre,
A garland red with roses bound it;
Its strings were wreath'd with lambent fire
And amaranth was woven round it.

I saw her mid the realms of light,
In everlasting radiance gleaming;
Co-equal with the seraphs bright,
Mid thousand thousand angels beaming.

I strove to reach her, when, behold,
Those fairy forms of bliss Elysian,
And all that rich scene wrapt in gold,
Faded in air – a lovely vision!

And I awoke, but oh! to me
That waking hour was doubly weary;
And yet I could not envy thee,
Although so blest, and I so dreary.

And ask ye why these sad tears stream?
Alfred, Lord Tennyson, 1809–92

gewe-
6.Jahre
t. 1796

Dear pretty youth, unveil your eyes,
How can you sleep when I am by?
Were I with you all night to be,
Methinks I could from sleep be free.
Alas, my dear, you're cold as stone:
You must no longer lie alone.
But be with me my dear, and I in each arm
Will hug you close and keep you warm.

Dear Pretty Youth
Thomas Shadwell, 1642(?)–92

I dreamt a dream! What can it mean?
And that I was a maiden Queen
Guarded by an Angel mild:
Witless woe was ne'er beguiled!

And I wept both night and day,
And he wiped my tears away;
And I wept both day and night,
And hid from him my heart's delight.

So he took his wings, and fled;
Then the morn blushed rosy red.
I dried my tears, and armed my fears
With ten-thousand shields and spears.

Soon my Angel came again;
I was armed, he came in vain;
For the time of youth was fled,
And grey hairs were on my head.

The Angel
William Blake, 1752–1827

She stands as pale as Parian statues stand;
Like Cleopatra when she turned at bay,
And felt her strength above the Roman sway,
And felt the aspic writhing in her hand.
Her face is steadfast toward the shadowy land,
For dim beyond it looms the light of day;
Her feet are steadfast; all the arduous way
That foot-track hath not wavered on the sand.
She stands there like a beacon thro' the night,
A pale clear beacon where the storm-drift is;
She stands alone, a wonder deathly white;
She stands there patient, nerved with inner might,
Indomitable in her feebleness,
Her face and will athirst against the light.

A Study (A Soul)
Christina Georgina Rossetti, 1830–1894

Come to me in my dreams, and then
By day I shall be well again!
For so the night will more than pay
The hopeless longing of the day.

Come, as thou cam'st a thousand times,
A messenger from radiant climes,
And smile on thy new world, and be
As kind to others as to me!

Or, as thou never cam'st in sooth,
Come now, and let me dream it truth,
And part my hair, and kiss my brow,
And say, My love why sufferest thou?

Come to me in my dreams, and then
By day I shall be well again!
For so the night will more than pay
The hopeless longing of the day.

Longing
Matthew Arnold, 1822–88

Twice or thrice had I loved thee,
Before I knew thy face or name;
So in a voice, so in a shapeless flame,
Angels affect us oft, and worshipped be;
Still when, to where thou wert, I came,
Some lovely glorious nothing I did see.

From Air and Angels
John Donne, 1572–1631

Far from the madding crowd's ignoble strife
Their sober wishes never learned to stray;
Along the cool sequestered vale of life
They kept the noiseless tenor of their way.

From Elegy Written in a Country Churchyard
Thomas Gray, 1716–71

She leads me on through storm and calm,
    My glorious Angel girt with light;
By dazzling isles of tropic balm,
    By coasts of ice in northern night.
Now far amid the mountain shades
    Her footprints gleam like golden fire,
And now adown the leafy glades
    I chase the music of her lyre.

From My Guide
George Francis Savage-Armstrong, 1845–1906

Angel spirits of sleep,
White-robed, with silver hair,
In your meadows fair,
Where the willows weep,
And the sad moonbeam
On the gliding stream
Writes her scatter'd dream:

Angel spirits of sleep,
Dancing to the weir
In the hollow roar
Of its waters deep;
Know ye how men say
That ye haunt no more
Isle and grassy shore
With your moonlit play;
That ye dance not here,
White-robed spirits of sleep,
All the summer night
Threading dances light?

Spirits
Robert Bridges, 1844–1930

Happy the man, and happy he alone,

He who can call today his own:

He who, secure within, can say,

Tomorrow do thy worst, for I have lived today.

Be fair or foul or rain or shine

The joys I have possessed, in spite of fate, are mine.

Not Heaven itself upon the past has power,

But what has been, has been, and I have had my hour.

Happy the Man
John Dryden, 1631–1700

Angels – a Journey Through their History

We may have our doubts, but the Church has never questioned the existence of angels. As early as the first ecumenical Council of Nicaea in 325, it was agreed that God created 'all creatures visible and invisible'. And all the Councils that followed, right up to Vatican I in 1870, strengthened believers' faith in these spiritual beings, in defiance of all rationalist trends. Even the continuing technological progress of our world could not shake the creed of the Church: God is almighty and makes use of his winged helpers. To make this clear, in 1951 Pope Pius XII declared that the Archangel Gabriel, who according to the Gospels announced to Mary that she was to be the mother of Jesus, was to be the patron of postal workers and of radio and television. So all our information culture, as well as our evening's entertainment, however frivolous, is under the protection of angelic wings.

Even without the justification provided by the Catholic Church, belief in angels seems to be stronger today than ever. Angels are successfully marketed in all forms as decorative accessories, and not only at Christmastime. Chubby-cheeked cherubs romp on pastel-coloured paper napkins, coffee mugs, handbags and umbrellas. Recently it has even been possible to buy T-shirts imprinted with wings at the height of the shoulder-blades. The glittering appliqué wings are of course intended ironically; 'no angel' would be likely to wear a midriff-revealing cropped top.

Seelig sind
die Todten, die
in dem HErren
sterben. Doch...

Dem Ande...
...sten Ehe...attin

Belief in a guardian angel, however, is taken very seriously, even if such an angel is called into service in a commercial for accident insurance. The idea of a personal guardian angel who watches over one's life is independent of belief in God and also independent of all religions. Recently, a whole range of advisers from all sorts of esoteric cults have been explaining in detail how one can make contact with one's personal guardian angel. 'Angelologists', a word derived from the Greek word 'angelos', or messenger, is the name given to these modern researchers, who offer to inform us about the number, origin, names and particular qualities of angels, even if they cannot supply any definite proof of their existence. 'Hogwash' is the verdict of critical rationalists, but for many people angels exist, and some are firmly convinced that they have met an angel at least once in their lives. Angels are a symbol of the concept that we are not alone on Earth.

If we survey the intellectual and artistic history of the last 2,000 years, it becomes clear that belief in angels, as well as their portrayal in art, has always been dependent on the current philosophical and aesthetic fashions of the era in question. Even the Bible does not provide a uniform picture. Statements about the appearance of angels and their visits to Earth vary considerably, The Old Testament mentions them only very rarely. In the story of creation, after the expulsion of Adam and Eve, God positions some cherubim 'with flaming swords' on guard outside the garden of Eden (Genesis 3:24), but most of the angels mentioned in the Old Testament are bringers of divine messages. Three angels in the shape of men appear to Abraham in his tent in Mamre, to tell him of the birth of his son Isaac (Genesis 18:2). Also anchored in the collective memory is the beautiful story of the dream of Jacob, who sees the angels climbing a long ladder to Heaven (Genesis 28:12). Only in the New Testament are the closer circumstances of their visits described in much greater and more spectacular detail. In the Gospel of Luke, the angel who announces the birth of the child Jesus to the sleeping shepherds in the field comes to Earth as an apparition of light, while the heavenly hosts celebrate the joyful event with their singing over the meadows of Bethlehem (Luke 2:8–20). Matthew also dramatically describes the 'angel of the Lord' who rolls back the stone at the entrance to Christ's tomb as having a countenance like 'lightning' and 'raiment white as snow' (Matthew 28:3).

After the Resurrection of Christ, angels are mentioned in the Bible not only as bringers of joyful news, but also, more frequently, as interpreters of the divine plan of salvation. They inform the women standing helplessly around the empty cave about the Resurrection of Christ, and describe Christ's Ascension into Heaven to the remaining apostles (Acts 1:10–12). In addition they are now responsible for the protection of the apostles and the young Christian community. When the disciples of Jesus are taken captive at the beginning of their preaching mission, an angel comes to free them (Acts 5:19).

We learn from the book of Revelation what tasks God has assigned to his angels on the Day of Judgement. Suddenly the beautiful spirit beings no longer appear in such a calm and helpful guise. With the sound of trumpets they bring the wrath of God upon the world and release countless disasters. The angels of the four winds bring devastating storms, and other angels pour out apocalyptic plagues upon humanity, transforming the earth into a place of horror; blood flows in the oceans, rivers cease to flow, the sun grows dark, and hail and a mighty earthquake destroy cities great and small, such as the mythical Babylon, and eventually human life.

In the early 6th century, the theologian Dionysius the Areopagite wrote his study of angels, *The Celestial Hierarchy*, based on the book of Revelation and the epistles of the apostle Paul. His main concern was to establish the order of precedence of the various groups of angels. Dionysius defined a hierarchy of angels on nine levels, which he subdivided into three main groups. The angels of the first level, the Seraphim, Cherubim and Thrones, live in the immediate vicinity of God and praise him ceaselessly. The second category of angels is formed by the so-called Dominations, Virtues and Powers, and the third group consists of the Principalities, Archangels and Angels. The last group are those who take up contact with humans, because they are considered to be guardians of all physical things. Even Thomas Aquinas (c. 1225–74), one of the most important scholars of the Middle Ages, adopted Dionysius' teaching more than 700 years later. In his text *Summa Theologica* Aquinas also tries to prove the existence of angels according to the rules of logic. Since an imperfect species always implies a more perfect one, one could argue as follows for the existence of angels: since there are living creatures below humankind, without intellect, such as animals, there must also be purely intellectual beings which have no bodies, which are above mankind.

The diffusion of the scholastic doctrine of angels and its mass impact during the Middle Ages can be attributed, not only to theologians and church historians, but also to the Italian poet Dante Alighieri (1265–1321) and his *Divine Comedy*. In his description of the heavenly

Paradise, which has been graphically illustrated from the Renaissance to the present day by artists such as Botticelli, Blake and Doré, the various choirs of angels spin round a central point in nine graduated spheres. In the Middle Ages, people were convinced that the whole cosmos was influenced by angelic powers, and that God had assigned a personal angel to every creature – whether human being, animal or plant.

Although theologians have defined angels as pure intellectual beings, artists have tried to create as precise an image of them as possible. Probably the earliest representation of an angel dates from the 2nd century BC and is in the Priscilla catacomb in Rome. As can be seen in the fresco in the subterranean burial chamber, in this early phase of Christian art, angels are still depicted without any special attributes, as adult males in white tunics. They wear sandals on their feet, but they have no wings. Not for another couple of hundred years did wings become indispensable for angels in the visual arts. Painters and sculptors clearly could no longer imagine these commuters between Heaven and Earth without the necessary aids to flying. After all, the predecessors of angels in classical antiquity were equipped with the wings of birds either great or small. The Greek god Hermes usually wears a winged cap or a pair of winged boots to assist him on his journey from the Olympus of the gods down to Hades. And the pagan figures of the goddesses of victory of ancient

Rome, of which more will be said later, could rise into the air only by means of powerfully beating wings.

Since the 5th century, a fine pair of wings has been the constant trademark of angels in art. It is only their clothing that is adapted to the current cultural climate or the changing times. In Byzantine times, the delicate youths of Roman catacomb paintings are transformed into stern men wearing costly garments, more appropriate for an emperor or king than for a devoted servant of God. At the time of the Crusades, in the 12th century, the Archangel Michael was often portrayed as a contemporary knight in chain mail, with shield and spear. Moreover, these supernatural beings now become humanized in art. Angels suddenly express emotions. In 13th-century Italian altarpieces they are clearly rejoicing in the birth of Jesus, or showing heart-rending grief at his burial.

The extensive metamorphosis experienced by the image of the angel in early modern times is unique in

the history of Christian iconography. First of all, the experiment-loving artists undertook the radical rejuvenation of the divine messengers. Giotto, in 1305, was the first to paint an unclothed child angel, in his frescoes in the Arena chapel in Padua, and since then it has been impossible to imagine art history without them. Chubby putti now pose in most altarpieces and church frescoes, not only as cute playmates for the child Jesus, but also, as in Raphael's famous painting of the Sistine Madonna in the Dresden Gemäldegalerie, as faithful companions of Mary, the mother of God.

Even more incisively, however, the gradual change of gender of angelic beings is portrayed in art – the serious young men first become androgynous musicians, then delightful young girls with flowers in their hair, who today are characteristic of our image of angels. Artists such as Fra Angelico and Alessandro Botticelli painted girl angels of breathtaking beauty, to represent appropriately the divine origin of angels. But even this delicate ideal of beauty could not be maintained for

long. The more sumptuous art became in the Baroque era, the more robust became the bodies of the angels. A good example of this new sensual aesthetic are the angels of Rubens, whose fleshy arms and legs dangle exhibitionistically from sunset-tinged mountainous clouds. In the 18th century, on the other hand, sweet child angels in white stucco were in great demand. They were placed at strategically favourable places in the painted and gilded inner rooms of churches, they hold candles and candelabra, support picture frames, open books, lift tabernacles and cavort exuberantly around altars.

Not until the Enlightenment was the belief in the heavenly messengers all but extinguished. From the time of the French Revolution, it was the rationalists who determined the intellectual climate. In the name of reason, angels were subjected by learned men to empirical examination and banished to the realms of fairytales and myth. Even Biblical accounts were questioned. God, it was said, had indeed created the world, but had then left it to its own devices, so that belief in guardian angels and messengers became obsolete. But only for a short time could authors such as the materialist philosopher Ludwig Feuerbach, who believed all divine beings to be products of the human imagination, banish the spell of these supernatural beings. The romantic, nostalgic image of the winged spirits between two worlds proved indestructible. In

bridge over a raging waterfall. The justification for this glowing veneration of guardian angels lies in the story of Tobias and the Archangel Raphael, told in the Apocrypha of the Old Testament. In order to collect a debt, the blind man Tobit sends his son Tobias on a long journey. The Archangel Raphael not only shows the boy the right way, but also heals Tobit's blindness.

Protestant Victorian England it was the Pre-Raphaelites who unwaveringly continued to pursue the cult of angels. Bewitching creatures, halfway between elves and angels, romp in their paintings, to be distinguished from the sensual women of the mythological pictures only by their wings. In the Germany of the Biedermeier era, angels are incorporated with equal lack of consideration for ecclesiastical or philosophical teachings into the personal mythology of the aspiring bourgeoisie of the industrial age of the 1870s. The printing firm of Hanfstaengl in Munich was able to turn this trend to their profit, and from 1850 they put on the market inexpensive art reproductions and photogravures with fairy-like angel scenes. In a format suitable for the living room, they were intended to warn the observer against offending bourgeois moral ideals. Images of guardian angels, hung on the walls of children's rooms, were particularly popular. Tall angels with giant wings hold their protective hands over children, doll-like in appearance, who have somehow reached the edge of a dreadful precipice, or a crumbling

One of the most frequently reproduced guardian angel scenes of the 19th century was Wilhelm von Kaulbach's design 'To God' (1858). It shows an angel carrying a dead child over a romantic landscape to Heaven. The idea of a winged being that accompanies the human soul to another world after death was already widespread in classical antiquity throughout the Mediterranean area. In the tomb paintings of the Egyptian pyramids we see birdlike creatures which lead the deceased into the hereafter. In Greek mythology, it is the god Hermes with his winged shoes who takes on the role of the conductor of souls, the so-called 'psychopomp'. The two mythical deities Hypnos (Sleep) and Thanatos (Death) are also represented in classical antiquity as winged children. Winged cupids are typical of the decorative design of Roman sarcophagi. These child angels, who carry upturned torches, surround reliefs with scenes from the life of the deceased. They are a popular death motif, which is repeatedly taken up again in the funerary art of the Renaissance and the Baroque.

The 19th century saw a positive invasion of European cemeteries by angels. These tomb angels, mostly carved in stone or cast in bronze or plaster by unknown artists, reflect the popular piety of the 19th century just as do the cheap prints of guardian angels. The cemetery angels are models of grief. But it would be wrong to suppose that their only function is to place before our eyes the entire repertoire of human mourning behaviour. Their sudden appearance is closely bound in with a new cemetery culture. Formerly laid out in monotonous fashion, these graveyards were now designed as landscape gardens, and the angels' role as figures identifying the deceased for survivors was now supplemented by the very secular task of marking the graves between the tall bushes and trees, so that they were not overlooked. In addition, cemetery angels give an indication of the economic status of the client who ordered them. Only well-heeled citizens could afford to pay a sculptor or stonemason to create a large sculpture to adorn a grave. The many angel figures in the Staglieno cemetery in Genoa, the Zentralfriedhof in Vienna and the Cimitero Monumentale in Milan are impressive testimony to the urge for prestige on the part of the wealthy, which has extended even beyond death.

The Russian writer Nikolai Gogol (1809–1852) wrote: 'The sorrow of an angel will set our poetry alight'. It is this poetry which Clemens Zahn's images attempt to capture. It was not he who placed a poppy or a champagne-coloured rose into the hands of the angel figures, to achieve an effective colour contrast. He photographed the sculptures just as he saw them on his expeditions to Vienna, Berlin, Genoa and Prague. The angels' faces are serious, their heads bowed. Some seem to be weeping, others to be brooding on the meaning of life. Certainly there are those who see nothing in their sensitive expressions beyond 'the mournful gaze of a dog from moss-covered eyes'. But most observers feel moved by them.

The cemetery angels show how many different possibilities there are for representing the heavenly messengers. Some have gigantic wings, others short stubby ones, some are small with puppy fat, some tall and muscular, some are male, some female. But one characteristic is particularly remarkable: many of them have an erotic charisma. With all due respect for the artistic freedom of sculptors, an obvious question presents itself: how is the proverbial purity of the angels reconciled with a sensually exposed body? The answer is to be found in the Old Testament and the Apocrypha. Angels have not always been seen as infallible spiritual beings, free from all earthly needs. The book of Enoch relates the story of the 'fallen angel', and in Genesis 6:1–4 we read that the 'sons of God' allowed themselves to be seduced by the beauty of the 'daughters of men' and fathered children who became giants and brought evil into the world. God's

punishment for the earthly transgressions of his heavenly messengers was not slow to follow. The 'fallen angels' were thrown into an angels' prison, and the lifetime of humankind was restricted to 120 years. The generally accepted concept of the pure spirituality and chastity of angels is thus only the positive side of the angelic myth. The less popular, negative side is however equally decisive in the Christian understanding of the world: Satan is a fallen angel, sent to Hell by God as punishment for his pride.

The winged Nikes or figures of Victory that have found their way into this book among the angels are also daringly clothed and placed in erotic contexts. They are considered iconographic forerunners of the angels and embody victory. In Greek mythology, they first appear as companions of the gods of victory, Zeus, Athena and Aphrodite. Later, in Roman classical antiquity, they were venerated as independent deities. The Nike of Samothrace in the Louvre is the best-known representative of her species in the visual arts. Although she is made of marble, we believe that she rules the air with her giant wings. A dynamic appearance with outspread wings is typical of the image of the goddess of victory. In her outstretched hand she usually holds a victor's laurel wreath, which in Clemens Zahn's photographs stands out in contrast against the blue sky. Just like the cemetery angels, the Nikes experienced an artistic renaissance in the Neo-classical era and in the 19th century. In Berlin, two urban landmarks were crowned with sculptures of Victory. In 1793 the sculptor Johann Gottfried Schadow set up his quadriga with a figure of Victory at the Brandenburg Gate, and in 1873 Friedrich Drake placed on the top of the victory column that today stands in the Tiergarten a golden statue of a goddess of victory, known affectionately to Berliners as 'Goldelse'.

Victories and tomb angels embody an abstract idea. Using traditional imagery, they express the pain of mourning and the triumph of victory. Although both have wings, they can be distinguished by their body language and their attributes. Only in the 20th century do angels in painting and sculpture become abstract figures, springing from the artist's imagination. Many watercolours and drawings by Paul Klee on the theme of angels have been preserved. But his angels are hardly to be recognized as such. Rather, they resemble playful matchstick men and bear strange titles such as 'Forgetful Angel' and 'Angel, still ugly'. Walter Benjamin

interpreted Paul Klee's enigmatic 'Angelus Novus' (1920) with his eyes opened wide in terror as a symbol for his own philosophy of history: 'This is what the angel of history should look like. His face is turned towards the past, but he has been carried away by the storm of progress and become entangled in his own wings'.

Less heavy with symbolism and weighed down by thought are the angels who have appeared on cinema screens since the 1940s. In films, the angelic image of the beautiful young woman is predominant. For example, in Tom McLoughlin's 1987 comedy *Date with an Angel*, in which the beautiful Emmanuelle Béart could be admired, Béart has the tricky task of rescuing a young man who is doomed to die before his marriage to an egocentric bride. Most films about angels follow a similar pattern. The theme is a guilty person or an unhappy love affair which can be saved only with the help of an angel. The images of Heaven dreamed up by Hollywood for these romantic films programmed for a happy ending are fairly unimaginative. The backdrop is usually no more than a sea of white clouds. If angels come to earth, they are unobtrusively dressed. Male angels wear dark suits or elegant white three-piece costumes, while female angels are usually blonde and blue-eyed.

In films, angels are more beautiful, stronger and wiser than humans. In Brad Silberling's film *City of Angels* (1998), an angel named Seth (Nicholas Cage), despite his supernatural faculties, suffers from a serious identity crisis on falling in love with a mortal named Maggie (Meg Ryan). Seth yearns to experience an earthly relationship – to be able to feel, love and smell Maggie. Eventually, Seth gives up his angelic status to live through his love. The message that the film seeks to convey to us is simple: our earthly life is so alive and so beautiful that even a heavenly creature may sacrifice his immortality and his freedom for it.

Claudia Lanfranconi

Clemens Zahn's photographs were taken at the following locations:

Potsdam, Germany
pages 4/5, 36, 39, 129, 135

Vienna, Austria
pages 9, 10, 11, 18/19, 24, 25, 26/27, 42, 43, 44/45, 52, 54/55, 57, 62/63, 65, 66, 68/69, 71, 72, 73, 76, 77, 78, 82, 83, 85, 86, 88/89, 93, 94, 96/97, 102/103, 108, 116, 117, 124, 125, 130/131, 137, 140, 141, 142, 143, 146

Berlin, Germany
pages 12/13, 16, 17, 29, 41, 48/49, 50, 51, 60, 75, 95, 101, 104, 119, 120/121, 122, 136

Rapallo, Italy
page 14

Portofino, Italy
page 20

Genoa, Italy
pages 22, 23, 28, 30, 34/35, 47, 80, 111, 150

Rhodes, Greece
pages 61, 115, 139

Prague, Czech Republic
pages 58, 59, 106, 107, 148, 149

Hamburg, Germany
page 91

Munich, Germany
pages 98, 99

Santa Margherita, Italy
pages 112/113

Perchtoldsdorf, Austria
pages 126, 127

Trieste, Italy
page 144

Sagrado, Italy
page 145